AMAZING SCIENCE

LIGHTNING

AND OTHER

WONDERS OF THE SKY

Q.L. PEARCE
Illustrated by Mary Ann Fraser

Julian Messner

To Heather

Acknowledgment

With thanks to William A. Selby, Professor of Geography/Earth Sciences, Santa Monica City College (California), for his critical reading of the manuscript.

Library of Congress Cataloging-in-Publication Data
Pearce, Q.L. (Querida Lee)
    Amazing science. Lightning and other wonders of the sky / Q.L. Pearce ; illustrated by Mary Ann Fraser.
        p. cm.
    Bibliography: p.
    Includes index.
    Summary: introduces wonders of earth's atmosphere, including auroras, mirages, trade winds, dust storms, acid rain, meteor showers, sundogs and a host of other meteorological phenomena.
    1. Atmosphere–Juvenile literature. 2. Meteorological optics–Juvenile literature. [1. Atmosphere. 2. Meteorological optics. 3. Curiosities and wonders.] I. Fraser, Mary Ann, ill. II. Title. III. Title: Lightning and other wonders of the sky.
QC863.5.P43 1989   89-8322
551.5–dc20   CIP
                                                                   AC
    ISBN 0-671-68534-1 (lib. bdg.)
    ISBN 0-671-68648-8 (pbk.)

Published by Julian Messner, a division of
Silver Burdett Press, Inc., Simon & Schuster, Inc.
Prentice Hall Bldg., Englewood Cliffs, NJ 07632.

JULIAN MESSNER and colophon are trademarks of
Simon & Schuster, Inc.
Manufactured in the United States of America.

Lib. ed.:   10 9 8 7 6 5 4 3 2 1
Paper ed.:   10 9 8 7 6 5 4 3 2 1

Contents

The Sky Above   5
The First Atmosphere   7
The Color of Sky   9
Auroras   11
Lightning   13
Balls of Fire   15
Mirages   17
Air Currents   19
Towering Thunderclouds   21
Hail   23
Rainbows   25
Halos and Sundogs   27
Snowflakes   29
Tornado Alley   31
Dust Devils and Dust Storms   33
Killer Hurricanes   35
Deadly Fog   37
Acid Rain   39
Arctic Terns   41
Monarch Migration   43
Incredible Hummingbirds   45
Weaverbirds   47
The Hoatzin   49
Imposter Eggs   51
Fireflies and Glowworms   53
The Zodiacal Light   55
Shooting Stars   57
Visitor from Space   59
Earth's Weirdest Weather   61
Tomorrow's Atmosphere   62

For Further Reading   63
Index   64

The Sky Above

The sky holds many wonders. Curtains of colored lights dance high in the air above the poles. Huge, dark clouds drop chunks of ice the size of golf balls on the ground. Close to Earth's surface, fantastic birds and insects flutter and wheel through the air.

If it weren't for the atmosphere, there would be no life on our planet. Earth's atmosphere is a sea of air more than 300 miles deep. Near the planet's surface, the atmosphere provides the air we breathe and traps heat. Its constantly moving winds spread this warmth across the planet. Our weather takes place in the troposphere, a ten-mile-high layer of air directly above the Earth's surface. The troposphere contains nearly eighty percent of the mass of the atmosphere and almost all of Earth's water vapor.

The atmosphere also protects us from harm. High in the sky, between ten and thirty miles above the surface, is the stratosphere. Within this level, a layer of ozone (a form of oxygen) absorbs, and protects us from, dangerous ultraviolet rays from the sun.

The atmosphere helps us to communicate as well. Above the stratosphere is the ionosphere, a layer of gases that begins about 30 miles above the Earth and stretches upward to 300 miles high. Within this region, certain radio waves are bounced back to Earth. These radio waves carry messages from one part of the planet to another. It is here in the ionosphere that the beautiful auroras, Earth's most dazzling light displays, are formed. From lovely auroras to strange birds to bizarre weather, this book will introduce you to the many wonders of the incredible sky above.

The First Atmosphere

When astronauts finally land on Mars, they will need special equipment to help them breathe. That's because the Martian atmosphere is deadly to humans. A few billion years ago, the first atmosphere around our own Earth would have been just as deadly. On the hot, young planet, volcanoes released many different gases that helped to form the early atmosphere. This steamy mixture included water vapor, carbon dioxide, ammonia, and methane gas, but it contained little or no oxygen. Without oxygen, life as we know it could not exist on this planet.

How, then, did oxygen first come into the atmosphere? Perhaps oxygen found its way into the air when ultraviolet radiation from the sun split atmospheric water molecules into their separate parts: hydrogen and oxygen. As Earth cooled over millions of years, other molecules in the air also reacted with radiation, with each other, and with the surface of the planet. Deadly gases were absorbed or altered, and the atmosphere continued to change (it is still changing even today). Water vapor condensed onto dust particles in the air, thus producing the first rain clouds. It probably rained continuously for many thousands of years, and slowly oceans began to form.

Protected in the young seas, the first plantlike algae (AL·jee) appeared about three billion years ago. Through photosynthesis, the algae added to the supply of oxygen in the atmosphere. As green plants do today, the algae used sunlight, carbon dioxide, and water to make food. The leftover material, oxygen, was released into the air. Over time, the Earth, unlike any other planet in our solar system, became a living planet.

Earth's original atmosphere was a poisonous mixture
of carbon dioxide, ammonia, and methane gas.

The Color of Sky

The sky above is always changing. On a clear day, it may be a lovely shade of robin's egg blue. It may look brilliant red at sunset, or velvety black at night. But would you guess that air is actually colorless? Then why does the sky appear blue or red? Because of sunlight.

White sunlight is actually made up of the seven colors of the rainbow: red, orange, yellow, green, blue, indigo, and violet. All light is a form of energy that travels to your eye in continuous waves, much like waves on an ocean. Each color has a different wavelength (the distance between the top of one wave to the top of the next). Red has the longest wavelength, and violet has the shortest. Over the same distance, then, there would be fewer long waves of red light and more short waves of violet light. When rays of sunlight pass through the atmosphere, they bounce against gas molecules and dust particles in the air. The short violet and blue waves hit many more particles and thus are scattered most. Everywhere you look, bluish light is directed to your eye. That is why the sky appears to be various shades of blue.

As the sun rises or sets, light rays that reach you from the horizon pass through a thicker layer of atmosphere than do light rays reaching you when the sun is overhead, say, at noon. Rays of light at sunrise or sunset encounter many more dust and gas molecules as they travel to your eye. As a result, blue light hits many more particles and is scattered even more—so much so that the blue hasn't a chance to reach your eyes. The longer red rays, however, come in a straighter line to your eye and are scattered less, so the setting sun and surrounding sky look red. Once sunlight with all of its colors no longer fills the sky, the night sky appears black.

The beautiful colors of the sky disguise
the fact that air is actually colorless.

Auroras

In the cold, clear skies of the far north and far south, one can see one of the most incredible sights on Earth, the auroras. These glowing curtains of light can cover nearly half the night sky from east to west. In the Northern Hemisphere, this is called the *aurora borealis* (uh·ROR·uh bor·ee·AL·us), which in Latin means "northern dawn." In the Southern Hemisphere, it is the *aurora australis* (ah·STRAY·lus), or "southern dawn." Most people call them the northern and southern lights.

The display begins with a greenish-white, wavy arc of light that lasts for a few hours. Then suddenly the lower edges begin to glow with shimmering sprays of pink, red, and purple. For a few moments the entire sky may be filled with dancing lights that slowly fade, leaving behind a dim glow. Though an aurora may sometimes seem to be very close, it is never closer than thirty-five miles high, and its top may be 155 miles high.

Where do these beautiful lights come from? Like a rainbow, the source of an aurora is the sun. The sun sends out streams of particles, known as the solar wind, into space. Our Earth is like a huge magnet surrounded by an invisible magnetic field, called the magnetosphere. Electrons in the solar wind are trapped by this magnetosphere. The electrons are then attracted to the poles, where they are funneled toward the Earth. As the speeding electrons get closer to the planet, they collide with atoms in the upper atmosphere. Each collision gives off a little electrical discharge, which we see as light. Millions of these discharges produce an aurora. The electrical power produced within an aurora is more than that used in the entire United States in a year.

The luminous pinks, greens, and reds of an aurora may fill the entire night sky.

Lightning

Lightning strikes the Earth about 100 times per second. In the time it takes you to read this sentence, more than 300 bolts will have struck somewhere on the Earth.

Actually, you can think of lightning as a huge spark from a cloud. Because of the incredible amount of energy in a thundercloud, ice and water particles are constantly being forced up and down, whipping past each other. The friction created as particles pass each other produces strong electrical currents. The charged particles separate, the positive ones collecting at the top of the cloud and the negative ones at the bottom. When the negative charge builds up, it may pass down to the Earth below. First, a "leader" stroke no wider than a pencil snakes down from the cloud almost to the ground. A "streamer" of electrons rises from the ground to meet the leader. When the two join, a "return" stroke hits the Earth, and we see a bolt of lightning.

Lightning bolts may reach temperatures five times hotter than the surface of the sun. They have even been known to melt the nails in a building and to cook potatoes growing in fields. A stroke of lightning lasts for only a few millionths of a second, but it delivers enough energy to run a 100-watt light bulb for three months. Lightning is also very fast and travels up to 87,000 miles a second. If it could reach the moon, it would take only two and a half seconds to get there. Our astronauts took three days to reach the moon!

Contrary to what you may have heard, lightning *can* strike the same place twice. Ray Sullivan, a park ranger, has been struck a record seven times. On one particular strike his watch melted. Lightning has knocked him out, caused him to lose a toenail, and burned his hair off.

These huge, powerful lightning bolts blaze through the sky at 87,000 miles per second.

Balls of Fire

What would you do if a hissing, fuzzy ball of white or colored light suddenly floated into your house? This is ball lightning, and scientists are not really sure what it is, or even if it exists. Many people, however, claim to have seen it. Eyewitnesses say the grapefruit-sized ball lightning drifts a few feet above the ground for several seconds, then disappears quietly or even explodes. One woman was cooking dinner when ball lightning floated down her chimney and slowly crossed the kitchen floor. It slid out of the door to the barn and then blew up, burning down the barn. In 1938, a pilot claimed that during a flight, ball lightning entered the cockpit of his plane, burned off his eyebrows, and then blew up in a puff.

If ball lightning does exist, computers predict that it would have the brightness of a 1,000-watt bulb (that's ten times brighter than the light bulb in an average reading lamp). Its core temperature would be between 6,000° and 10,000° Fahrenheit, or as hot as the surface of the sun. The strange ball of fire seems to be somehow related to common lightning. It may form in small pockets of air heated by a lightning bolt.

St. Elmo's fire is another strange form of lightning. Named for the patron saint of fire, it is a type of electrical discharge that crackles and clings to chimney tops, the wings of airplanes, and the masts of ships. It occurs when an object becomes charged with static electricity, usually during a storm. The electricity discharges as ghostly fingers of light at the tip of that object—the mast of a ship, for example. Sailors of old believed that St. Elmo's fire was a sign of good luck and would protect them at sea.

A strange sight—the static lightning of
St. Elmo's fire on a ship at sea.

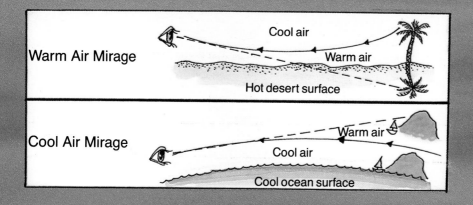

Warm Air Mirage

Cool air

Warm air

Hot desert surface

Cool Air Mirage

Warm air

Cool air

Cool ocean surface

Mirages

Have you ever seen water shimmering on the road ahead and then found that it was not really there? The water was just a mirror image of the sky. It was a mirage (muh·RAZH).

Mirages are tricks of light. A mirage occurs when light passing through one air layer to another is bent, just as light passing from air into water is bent. (You can see this effect for yourself if you put a pencil in a glass of water and then look at it from the side.) Air of different temperatures forms different layers. In a hot desert, for example, the air layer near the ground is warmer and lighter than the air layer above it. Light rays bend toward the cooler air layer. Some of the light reflecting off a desert palm tree would go directly to your eye, and you would see the object as it normally appears. Some of the light would also go toward the hot ground. This light would bend upward toward the cooler layer of air above. When this light reaches your eye, you would see an upside-down tree below the real tree.

Mirages occur at sea, too. Here, the air layer closest to the water is usually colder than the air layer above it. As a result, sea mirages, which are right side up and above the object, are different from desert mirages, which are upside down and below the object. The light reflected from a ship, for example, bends downward when it reaches a warm air layer above. You see the image of the ship above the water.

Amazing effects can occur when warm air is sandwiched between two layers of colder air. In Italy, over the Straits of Messina, you can see a stack of three villages piled on top of each other in the sky. This famous mirage, called the Fata Morgana, is often so clear that people dressed in white are sometimes seen walking in the streets.

Layers of warm and cool air create magical scenes—like this mirage at sea.

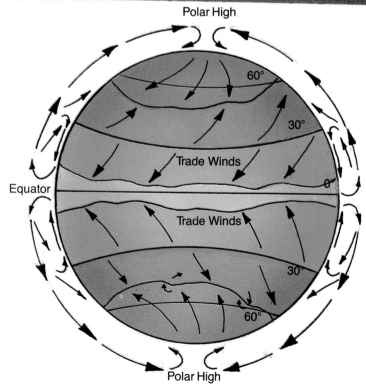

Polar High

Equator

60°

30°

Trade Winds

0°

Trade Winds

30°

60°

Polar High

Air Currents

Between thirty degrees north and south of the equator, the gentle trade winds blow at about twelve miles per hour. These reliable, steady winds provided much of the sailing power for Christopher Columbus's voyage of discovery from Europe to the New World. There are two trade wind belts, one just north of the equator and one just south. They are part of worldwide circular patterns of airflow.

These patterns exist because of the uneven heating of the Earth by the sun. Polar regions are warmed the least, and the equatorial region is warmed the most. At the equator, the warm air rises, creating a calm belt known as the doldrums. As air moves away from the equator toward the poles, much of it sinks and becomes more dense. In this way, belts of high pressure known as the horse latitudes are created. These belts are found at about thirty degrees above and below the equator. The weather here is hot, dry, and still.

Eventually, the dense air flows back toward the equator, replacing the warm, rising air of the doldrums and starting the circulation cycle again. It was once estimated that 200 million tons of air from the Northern Hemisphere alone flows toward the equator every second. That movement of air is felt as wind. At the two trade wind belts, the spin of the Earth causes the wind to blow toward the west.

Air currents flowing away from the horse latitudes toward the poles give rise to less predictable winds–the prevailing westerlies. At about sixty degrees north and south of the equator, these warmer westerlies meet the cold polar easterlies. The clash of these great masses of air creates some of the strongest winds on the planet. In the Southern Hemisphere, these winds often reach 100 miles per hour.

Without the gentle trade winds, Christopher Columbus might never have reached America.

Towering Thunderclouds

How many thunderstorms would you guess bombard the Earth each year? Would you guess in the thousands? The correct answer is over sixteen million! A total of nearly two billion gallons of rain falls to Earth each year, and it comes from some of the tallest clouds in the sky—the cumulonimbus (kew·mew·loh·NIM·bus), or thunderclouds. These huge mounds can tower up to ten miles into the atmosphere.

A thundercloud forms when warm, moist air rises and cools. Cooled water vapor condenses onto particles in the air, forming water droplets. The warm air continues to rush upward, creating powerful updrafts. Water droplets falling within the cloud produce drag, which creates equally powerful downdrafts. As water gathers in the cloud, it becomes so heavy that it falls as rain. A single large thundercloud may contain more than 150,000 tons of water—enough to fill a dozen Olympic-sized swimming pools.

In 1959, a pilot experienced what it is like to be a raindrop. In an emergency, he was forced to parachute from his plane at 47,000 feet into a huge thundercloud. It was exactly six o'clock. He thought to himself that it would take only about ten minutes to fall to Earth. He had no idea what was in store for him. After entering the cloud, the unlucky pilot was bounced up and down by the powerful, shrieking winds. He was rolled and slammed within the violent cloud. That is not surprising, since gusts in a thundercloud can reach sixty-five miles per hour. Barely able to breathe, the pilot feared he would drown because there was so much water in the cloud. He finally made it safely to Earth. His watch read 6:40. He had spent forty minutes in the heart of a thundercloud, and it was a ride he would never forget.

These black, water-filled thunderclouds
can tower up to ten miles into the air.

Hail

You may think that the summer is an odd time for ice to fall from the sky, but hailstorms are most common in August. This is because the huge clouds, or thunderclouds, that produce hailstones generally form in the summer. These thunderclouds can tower more than ten miles high, where temperatures may be as low as -100° Fahrenheit.

Hail forms on dust particles or ice crystals within a thundercloud. In order for hail to form, the crystals must remain within the cloud until they reach the proper size. When crystals fall through the cloud, water droplets freeze onto the particles. The warm, strong updrafts common in summer carry the icy pellets back up into the cloud to repeat the process. A hailstone makes several round trips before it is heavy enough to fall to Earth.

Farmers call hail the "white plague." The largest hailstone ever found weighed almost two pounds and was more than seventeen inches around. Hailstones can fall to Earth at speeds up to 100 miles per hour, and if large enough, they can flatten crops, dent car roofs, and break windows. The falling ice causes about one billion dollars' worth of crop damage in the United States every year. In 1985, a hailstorm in Cheyenne, Wyoming, killed twelve people and dropped six inches of ice on the ground.

The most unusual and tragic of all hailstones fell in 1930. German glider pilots were trying to ride the updrafts in storm clouds. Two pilots lost control of their planes, which became caught in the strong updrafts and began to break apart. One pilot parachuted to safety. The other was carried up into the cloud, where he was soon covered with ice. He fell to his death as a human hailstone.

The "white plague" to farmers, hailstones can fall to Earth as fast as 100 miles per hour.

White light

Water drop

Rainbows

Have you ever seen a prism split a beam of sunlight into many colors? Well, raindrops are like tiny prisms. If the sun breaks through the clouds after a rain, stand with it behind you and you will often see a beautiful colored arc in the sky . . . a rainbow.

When sunlight shines through the raindrops, it separates into its individual colors. The rainbow you see is the result of the light refracted (or bent) and reflected (or bounced back) by millions of raindrops. Because no two people can stand in exactly the same place at the same time, no two people see exactly the same rainbow. The colors are always in the same order, however. Red is at the top, then orange, yellow, green, blue, indigo, and finally violet at the bottom. You can remember these colors by remembering the name ROY G. BIV. Each letter in the name stands for a color in the rainbow, and the letters are in the correct order.

Most rainbows appear and disappear quickly, but one sighted in Wales after a gentle rain glistened in the afternoon sun for nearly three hours. Sometimes a fainter rainbow appears above the first. Known as a double rainbow, the colors in the upper arch will be reversed. You don't have to wait for rain to look for a rainbow, however. With the sun behind you, it is possible to see rainbows in the mists of a waterfall, the drops of a water fountain, or even in the spray of a garden hose. Unfortunately, the legendary pot of gold at the end of the rainbow is an impossibility. If you could see the whole rainbow at once, you would see why: A rainbow is actually a circle. It appears to be a half circle because the ground is in the way, and you are only seeing a part of it. From an airplane, you can view the entire rainbow ring.

It takes millions of tiny raindrops to turn sunlight into a sparkling rainbow.

Halos and Sundogs

There is an old saying that a ring around the moon means a storm is brewing. Even though it is not always true, there is good scientific sense behind this. The clouds that cause the moon's halo are sometimes a sign that a low pressure area is moving in. That means a change in the weather, usually accompanied by a storm.

A halo forms around the moon or sun when wispy, icy cirrus (SIR·us) clouds gather in the air. These clouds develop very high in the sky. They are usually so thin that the moon or sun can be seen through them, as through a veil. Light is bent by the ice crystals in the clouds, producing ghostly rings around the moon and pale bands of color around the sun, beginning with red on the inner edge. The most common sun halos are small rings that appear to be as wide as two fists held at arm's length (about six inches wide). They may be twice that width, but that is not as usual. Sometimes you may even see a double halo.

When the ice crystals are medium sized or larger, they may cause another unusual sight: sundogs. These often appear in pairs, one on each side of the outer edge of the sun's halo. They are bright patches of light, red on the inner side and yellow-white in the center. On the outer side, slender rays of white light shooting away from the sun form the sundogs' "tails." Sometimes, if conditions are just right, you may see sundogs and halos at the same time.

Never look directly at the sun! It is dangerous because your eyes can be damaged. If you want to look at a halo or sundog, use your hand to block the center of the sun and look at the streams of light around your hand. You will still be able to see a large part of these beautiful formations in the sky.

Light shining through ice crystals in the sky
produces a spectacular sight—halos and sundogs.

Snowflakes

Have you ever heard it said that no two snowflakes are alike? It's true. The shape of a snowflake depends on the air temperature and moisture content of the cloud in which it is formed. Snowflakes form as water vapor freezes onto ice crystals. Though all snowflakes are variations of a basic six-sided pattern, to look exactly alike two snowflakes would have to pass through the same conditions in the same order. Movements within the atmosphere make it unlikely this would happen. There may be a million different combinations of temperature and moisture the snowflakes might pass through during their formation.

Also, if the air near the ground is greater than 39° Fahrenheit, the snowflake usually turns into rain as it falls to Earth. During a storm in New York in 1958, it snowed on the top of the Empire State Building but rained on the streets below.

Cold weather doesn't always mean it's going to snow. There must also be moisture in the air. Thus, it may surprise you to learn that Antarctica, the coldest place on Earth, has little snowfall. The reason there is so much snow on the ground is because very little of it ever melts away. Visitors to the freezing, but dry, region often see a most unusual sight. The warm, moist air they breathe out immediately turns to snow in front of them and falls gently to the ground.

Snow is not always white. In parts of Canada and the western United States, snow has been known to be pale pink or mint green. Sometimes winds carry reddish soil into the air. This soil clings to the snowflakes, making them appear pink. Tiny plants called cryoplanktons, known to live on snow and ice, can make the snow appear green.

Of all the billions of snowflakes that fall to Earth, no two are exactly alike.

Tornado Alley

Do you remember the story of *The Wizard of Oz*? In it, a tremendous tornado carries Dorothy and her little dog Toto to a land far away. Dorothy lived in the central United States within an area known as Tornado Alley. From the Texas panhandle through Oklahoma, Kansas, Missouri, Nebraska, Iowa, and Illinois, this area is struck by at least 300 tornadoes per year. Several surrounding states—Minnesota, Indiana, Wisconsin, and South Dakota—are also battered by a high number of tornadoes each year.

In the United States, tornadoes occur most often when warm, wet air moving up from the Gulf of Mexico meets cool, dry air moving down from Canada. Huge thunderclouds build up (*tornado* is from a Spanish word meaning "thunderstorm"), then a funnel-shaped cloud spins downward to Earth. Tornado winds may whip around at speeds up to 400 miles per hour. If the funnel touches ground, it can cause great damage to anything in its path.

In 1931, a tornado in Minnesota sucked five eighty-ton cars of a passenger train into the air. It dropped them into a ditch, killing many of the passengers. The most destructive tornado to date hit a section of Tornado Alley in 1925. This terrible storm cut a 200-mile-long path through Missouri, Illinois, and Indiana. Nearly 700 people lost their lives, and the damage to property was in the millions of dollars.

Tornadoes are not limited to the central United States, nor do they always cause destruction. A tornado in Italy lifted a sleeping baby in its carriage. The child was lifted fifty feet up and set gently down more than 300 feet away. The baby was not only unharmed, it didn't even wake up.

A spinning tornado whips through Tornado Alley in the central United States.

Dust Devils and Dust Storms

Legends of the world's great deserts usually include tales of whirling demons howling across the sand. Dust devils are not evil spirits, but columns of warm air spiraling upward from the hot desert surface. Over a one-month period in 1962, researchers in an Arizona desert near Tucson counted more than 1,600 dust devils in one area. The scientists also discovered that these dry whirlwinds occur most often between 12:30 and 2:00 in the afternoon, when the desert sand is hottest. Most dust devils are gentle and last only a few minutes. But, some may become spinning columns hundreds of feet high, whirling at more than fifty miles per hour. One amazing dust devil in western Utah reached nearly a half mile into the sky and lasted for seven hours.

In North Africa, a seasonal desert wind of the Sahara, called a haboob, can raise huge walls of dust thousands of feet high. These incredible dust storms can be thick enough to block sunlight, turning a sunny day into twilight. The winds may carry dust from the Sahara high into the atmosphere, where it is often transported great distances. Once, bloodred rain fell on Locarno, Switzerland, 2,000 miles away. The snow on the Swiss Alps was pale pink. The Red Sea, which separates the Arabian Peninsula from the African continent, got its name partly because of the reflection of the red dust filling the desert sky.

There are dust storms on other planets, too. Each spring on Mars, great winds roar across the barren planet. These storms fill the atmosphere with red dust that can be seen from Earth, earning Mars the nickname "the red planet."

A whirling demon of hot sand, a dust devil
storms through a desert.

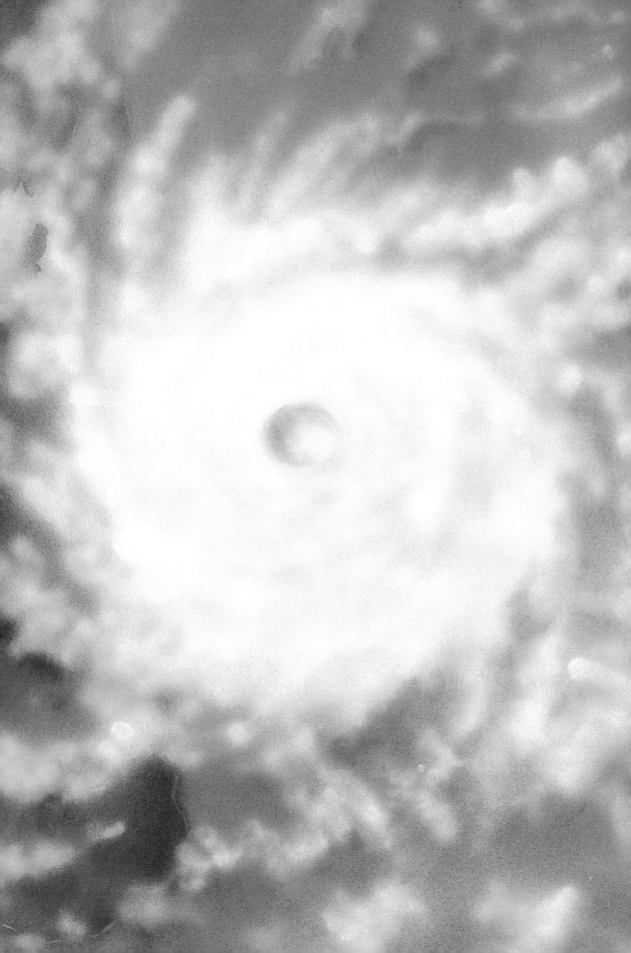

Killer Hurricanes

West of the international date line hurricanes are called typhoons. They are cyclones in the Indian Ocean and willy willies in Australian waters. But no matter what you call them, hurricanes are dangerous.

Hurricanes usually form near the equator in warm seas and move northwesterly. A tropical storm becomes a hurricane when its winds reach seventy-four miles per hour. However, a truly raging hurricane can have wind speeds up to 200 miles per hour. The storm can also produce a surge, or gigantic wave of water, that can be twenty feet high or more. The surge can be even more deadly than the winds. In 1970, a vicious hurricane surge hit the low-lying lands of Bangladesh, causing the deaths of thousands of people.

Hurricane winds and clouds spin around a calm center, called the eye of the storm. The eye can be five to thirty miles across. The wind speed inside the eye may drop to as little as ten miles per hour, sometimes even less. As the winds die down and the clouds part, the sun may even come out. But beware—this is one of the more dangerous parts of the storm. As the eye passes over, people are tempted to come out to look for and repair damage. Almost without warning, the other wall of the hurricane slams through with its howling winds and drenching rain.

The history of the discovery and settling of America is filled with tales of violent hurricanes. Many Spanish galleons loaded with gold were sunk in the fierce storms, and some of their treasure still lies on the bottom of the sea. A savage hurricane in 1609 even inspired a play by the great writer William Shakespeare. Based on a Latin word meaning "storm," it is called *The Tempest*.

With howling wind all around it,
the eye of the hurricane is calm and quiet.

Deadly Fog

In some ways, fog may be the most dangerous of all clouds. If thick enough, fog can prevent you from seeing more than a few feet in front of you. This has had disastrous results for airplanes and ships at sea trying to navigate. In 1977, thick fog contributed to the worst air disaster in history—two huge passenger jets crashed into each other on a runway in the Canary Islands.

London has always been known for its low-lying, thick fogs. These fogs are dense enough to be nicknamed pea-soupers. In 1952, one of these thick fogs became deadly. Cool air at the ground produced the fog, and a warm upper layer of air prevented any of it from blowing away. (This is called a temperature inversion.) Gas and smoke from factories and coal fires filled the still air. On December 5, a thick, yellow smog sat over the city. It was the type of fog you might expect to see in a horror movie, but it contained more to fear than make-believe monsters. The sulfur and other pollutants in the fog made it almost impossible to breathe. It was so cold and damp that more coal fires were lit, and the air became smoggier still. Even indoors there was no escape. The smog entered homes, making the walls dark with soot. Movie theaters had to close because audiences couldn't see the screens. Although the fog did not have the raging winds of a tornado or the destructive force of a hurricane, it proved deadlier than most of those terrible storms. Four thousand people died of diseases such as bronchitis and pneumonia brought on during the five days the fog lasted.

In 1952, London was buried
under a thick layer of deadly fog.

Acid Rain

The taste of lemon juice can make you pucker your lips and wrinkle your nose. It is the acid in the juice that makes it taste that way. Can you imagine rain as acidic as lemon juice? Rain forms when water vapor condenses onto particles in the air. Normally, these are dust, ash, or salt particles from the ocean or from dry salt flats. About 200 million tons of dust and one billion tons of sea salt find their way into the air every year. Once water vapor has condensed onto these particles, carbon dioxide from the air dissolves into the rain, forming a mild carbonic acid. Thus, normal rainwater is actually a very weak acid.

Unfortunately, other gases can combine with rainwater, too. Fumes from factories or cars can make rainwater dangerously acidic. Sulfur salts, given off when soft coal is burned to keep homes warm, also find their way into the atmosphere. From chimneys and smokestacks, these materials may rise high into the air and be carried great distances by winds. The ash and sulphuric salts eventually combine with water vapor and fall as rain. This acid rain, however, is thirty times more acidic than normal.

Acid rain can be very destructive. In Germany, more than 200,000 acres of valuable forests show damage from acid rain. In North America, fish populations in the lakes of Canada and the northeastern United States are dying as acid rain pollutes the water. This dangerous rain can ruin buildings and statues, too. In Athens, Greece, the birthplace of modern civilization, ancient monuments are crumbling. In fact, these buildings have suffered more damage over the past forty years than in the 2,000 years before.

Factories fill the air with dangerous gases,
making rain far more acidic than usual.

Migration path

Dark blue represents migration paths

Arctic Terns

The arctic tern is one of the world's champion voyagers. This bird travels more distance than any other migrating animal. In one year, it may journey 24,000 miles, a distance equal to one complete trip around the Earth.

The tern's summer breeding grounds stretch across the far northern reaches of North America, Europe, and Asia. When winter's chill creeps into the north, the terns all head for the antarctic. The travelers follow several migration paths south. Those terns that nested in western North America join up in Alaska and fly over the Pacific Ocean to Antarctica. Terns that nested in eastern North America cross the Atlantic Ocean and join other terns in Europe. Together they fly just south of the equator, where they break into smaller groups. Each group takes a different course, but when they reach Antarctica, they join for their winter feeding.

No one is sure how arctic terns choose their migration paths or find their way over such distances. They may use the position of the sun to guide them. However, these birds can navigate even in the dark, so perhaps they use the stars or Earth's magnetic field to find their way.

The tern holds another record besides that of long distance: It enjoys more sunshine per year than any other animal on Earth. This is because for about half the year, the North Pole points toward the sun. In fact, the summer sun at the North Pole never sets below the horizon and is nicknamed the "midnight sun." As the Earth moves in its orbit, it is the South Pole's turn to face the sun. Because the arctic tern flies from the "land of the midnight sun" in the north to the "land of long sunny days" in the south, the tern basks in about eight continuous months of daylight.

In a single year, the arctic tern may
travel enough miles to circle the globe.

Summer
range

Winter
range

Monarch Migration

If you see a lovely, orange and black monarch butterfly fluttering lazily through the sunny sky, you might never guess it is the long-distance champion of the insect world. Like many birds, monarch butterflies fly south in the fall and north in spring. The butterflies probably begin their southward trek when the days become shorter, signaling the coming winter. Some monarchs may fly all the way from southern Canada to their winter homes in California and Mexico, a journey of nearly 2,000 miles. They travel only during the day and at an average speed of about seven miles an hour.

Although bad weather and predators take their toll, millions of butterflies arrive in California and Mexico during October and November. They settle in various tree groves for several months of warm winter weather. In one particular eucalyptus grove in Santa Cruz, California, hundreds of thousands of butterflies arrive every year. In the area, October 9 is known as "Welcome Back Monarch Butterfly Day." To welcome the arriving travelers, there is a celebration that includes the appearance of "Monarch Man." Dressed as a giant butterfly, he swoops down from above on a cable. In Pacific Grove, California, the school children dress up to celebrate and march in the children's "Butterfly Parade."

The butterflies remain in the groves until the warm, sunny days of early spring. Then they begin the long return trip to the north, where they will lay their eggs and then die. Monarchs make this amazing flight with no leaders and no experience. In fact, the butterflies that fly south each year are the grandchildren, or even the great-grandchildren, of the insects that flew south the year before.

Every year, the fragile monarch crosses
nearly 2,000 miles over North America.

Planalto
hummingbird
nest

Incredible Hummingbirds

Not only does the hummingbird family include the world's smallest birds, it also includes the world's smallest warm-blooded animals of any kind. The tiniest of these birds is the Cuban bee hummingbird. At two inches long from beak to tail, it weighs only one-fifteenth of an ounce. Not all hummingbirds are tiny, however. The giant hummingbird of South America (giant for a hummingbird, that is) may grow to a length of eight inches.

These beautiful birds are among the world's most skillful fliers. Their wings move so fast they are almost invisible. Some hummingbirds beat their wings an incredible 4,500 times per minute! They can fly backwards, sideways, and even upside down–no other bird can do that. Hummingbirds are such good fliers that they can escape most predators. The tiny birds are not afraid to defend their nests, even against intruders many times their size. One courageous pair was seen protecting their little nest from a huge eagle that had flown too close. Still, even a hummingbird can be caught by surprise. The Cuban bee hummingbird is so small it has been known to be captured by the praying mantis, a very large insect.

The colorful hummingbird is also an excellent nest builder. It gathers many materials, such as grass, moss, and leaves, and weaves them with delicate threads of spider silk. One of the most unusual nests is built by the planalto hermit. It attaches its nest to the underside of a branch by long strands of grass and fibers. To balance the nest, the little bird adds a long column of pebbles on one side. The nest is not only level, but also well out of the reach of egg-stealing predators.

Tiny broad-tailed hummingbirds bravely defend their nest against a golden eagle.

Weaverbirds

Did you ever think of a bird as an architect? Well, weaverbirds are the great builders of the bird world. They are called "weavers" because of their nest-building talents. Amazingly, all weaverbirds are born with this talent. Even young weaverbirds separated at birth from their parents know how to weave. They are also intelligent birds. Human trainers have taught Indian Baya weaverbirds to string beads with a needle and cord. An old legend says that these birds even weave fireflies into their nests to scare away snakes.

Some weaverbirds, such as the male red-billed Quelea (kwee·LEE·uh) of Africa, build individual nests. The male Quelea tears away leaves in long strips, then winds the strips around small branches or twigs in a tree. He uses his feet to hold the strips down while he weaves them with his beak. He even knots certain strands. This busy bird works until he has made a ring between two small twigs, like a round doorway. Building outward from the ring, he weaves a comfortable sac with the open ring as the only entrance.

Social weaverbirds build huge communal nests. They choose a tree and all begin work on an enormous straw roof. The roof may be fifteen feet high and ten feet wide. Then, each bird builds individual nest chambers under the roof. This "condo in the sky" may be home to up to 300 birds.

Although most weaverbirds build excellent nests, there are exceptions. The house sparrow is a weaverbird, but it builds a small, untidy nest of grass and straw. Widowbirds are members of this family, but they don't build a nest at all. Like the cuckoo, they prefer to lay their eggs in the nests of other birds.

Up to 300 weaverbirds build and live in these huge "condos in the sky."

The Hoatzin

In the hot, swampy basin of the Orinoco River of Venezuela live some very unusual creatures. Among them is a strange relative of the common chicken–the hoatzin (wat·SEEN). This remarkable bird lives in permanently flooded forests, where it finds the marsh plants, tiny crabs, and fish it eats. During the hot part of the day, the odd bird rests in the trees. At night, it hops through the branches hissing and uttering loud, hoarse cries. When it takes to the sky, the hoatzin flies rather clumsily in a series of short flights.

About the size of a large hawk, the hoatzin is so unusual that scientists have put it in an order all by itself. For one thing, the hoatzin has something that very few birds have . . . eyelashes. It also has an unmistakable odor. Some people say you can smell the hoatzin's husky scent long before you catch sight of the bird. The odor must not be very pleasant, because the creature has been nicknamed "the stinking pheasant."

The most incredible thing about the hoatzin is the way it looks as a chick. The young bird looks very much like the ancient reptile, archaeopteryx (ar·kee·OP·tuh·riks). That small feathered creature lived during the age of the dinosaurs. Like the archaeopteryx, the young hoatzin is born with two sharp claws on its wings. The strong hooks help the chick to grasp branches and climb in the trees. It will lose these claws by the time it is an adult. The little bird can also swim and dive as well as any seal. When the chick is frightened, it may dive from high on a branch into the swampy water below.

A bizarre cousin of the chicken, the hoatzin
is born with tiny claws on its wings.

Imposter Eggs

Cuckoos may be among the biggest freeloaders ever. They don't bother building nests–they just lay their eggs in the nests of other birds.

Perhaps the best example of the cuckoo's nest-stealing activity is the work of the bronze cuckoo. These colorful birds of the South Pacific breed in New Zealand. The female lays its eggs in the nest of a bird called a flycatcher. The parent cuckoos then fly away, leaving the little flycatcher to hatch and raise the baby birds. When grown, the young cuckoos fly over the ocean to Australia, and then northward to the Solomon Islands. Here, they manage to find many of the adult cuckoos that had made the trip from New Zealand many months before. The young cuckoos will have flown a trip of more than 2,000 miles, with no way of knowing the course ahead of time. Even stranger is the fact that they were raised by the flycatcher, a bird that doesn't migrate at all.

While the bronze cuckoo usually chooses the flycatcher to be foster parent, the European cuckoo is not very particular about whom it chooses to raise its eggs. Over 150 different kinds of birds have been known to raise the chicks of the European cuckoo. Female cuckoos watch as other birds build nests. When another bird lays her eggs and then leaves the nest to feed, the female cuckoo sneaks in. She gets rid of one egg (often by eating it) and lays one of her own in its place. Sometimes the nest owner realizes the trick. It may throw out the one cuckoo egg or even desert the nest. If the foster mother is fooled and cares for the imposter egg, the cuckoo hatches a day or two before its nestmates. Amazingly, though blind and featherless, it quickly throws out the other eggs! In this way, it gets rid of competition for food.

Another bird is often tricked into incubating and then raising a cuckoo chick.

Adult

Eggs

Pupa

Larva

Fireflies and Glowworms

A long time ago, Indians of the Caribbean didn't need lanterns when they walked through the jungle at night. They used insects. Of course, these were no ordinary insects, but members of a family that we generally call fireflies. Their light was so bright that when the clever natives attached the insects to their toes they could see the path ahead. They even used cages filled with fireflies to light their homes. The Indians had a lot of fireflies to choose from—in Jamaica alone there are at least fifty different kinds. One kind has green headlights it uses when walking and orange taillights it uses when flying.

The flash of light fireflies produce is a chemical reaction. A lovely sight in the evening sky, the twinkling lights are used for courting. The female flashes her light to attract males. The male answers with his own flashing light. Scientists have been able to attract males to light bulbs that had the same glow, number, and pattern of flashes of a female firefly. A firefly's glimmer is so persistent it may even continue for a short time after the insect dies. One scientist thought he had discovered a new type of animal when he found a frog with a glowing stomach. It turned out that the frog had recently eaten a meal of fireflies!

A true firefly glows at all stages in its life. Glowworms, however, are the young of insects that will not produce light as adults. In New Zealand, there is an area in Waitomo Cave called Glowworm Grotto. Millions of insect larvae hang from the ceiling of the cave. They produce so much greenish-blue light that you could read this book in there. However, when frightened by sound, the little insects will "turn off." A cough or sneeze can plunge the grotto into darkness.

These unusual fireflies twinkle like miniature stars in the night sky.

The Zodiacal Light

After the sun has set, the sky still holds many wonders. One by one, the stars begin to glitter against the darkness. At times, a glowing starry river known as the Milky Way stretches across the night sky. If you look very carefully, you may also see a soft glimmer low in the sky. This mysterious shining patch is called the zodiacal (zoh·DY·uh·kul) light.

Long ago, our ancestors saw patterns in certain star groups and gave these groups, or constellations, names. Twelve major constellations appear along the apparent route taken by the sun during the day. Many of these star groups are named for animals, and so they are called signs of the *zodiac,* which comes from a Latin word meaning "zoo." The zodiacal light appears in the general area of the sky where the signs of the zodiac meet the horizon.

About two hours after sunset you may see a fuzzy patch of light above the western horizon. This western zodiacal light slowly fades, until, by midnight, it is barely visible at all. An hour or two after midnight, the first glow of the eastern zodiacal light becomes visible. It grows a little brighter as the early morning wears on, until it is drowned out by the first rays of sunrise. The zodiacal light is not easy to see. You are most likely to see it from a hilltop on a very dark, moonless night, well away from city lights.

Scientists are not sure what causes the zodiacal light, but many believe it is sunlight reflected back to Earth from a cloud of dust and tiny asteroids far out in space. These particles may be all that remains of the huge cloud from which our solar system formed more than four billion years ago.

The pale glow of the zodiacal light is best seen away from the glare of city lights.

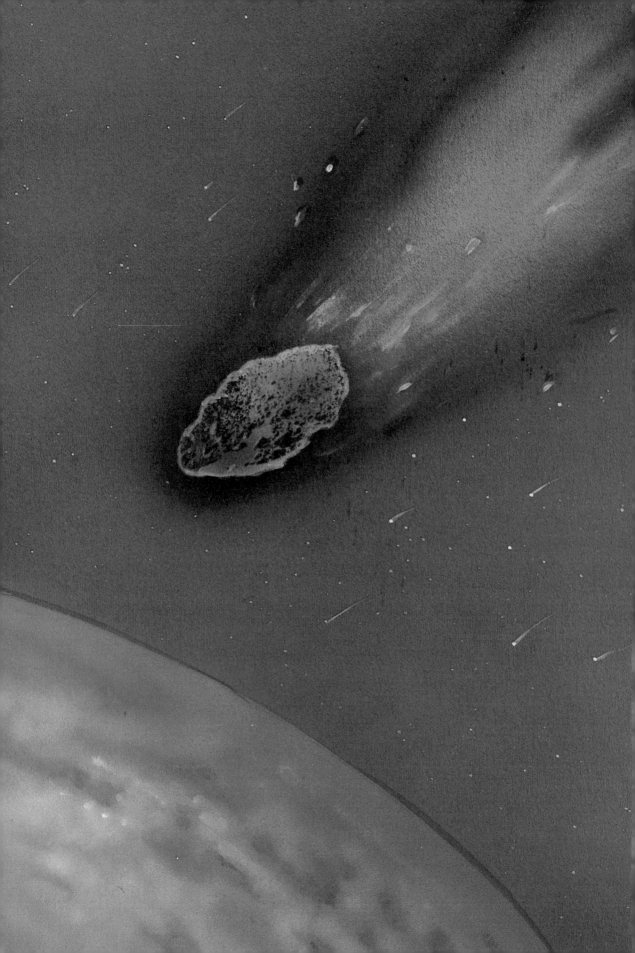

Shooting Stars

Have you ever gazed up into the night sky and seen a bright flash of light? It was probably a meteor, or "shooting star." Actually, meteors are not stars but streaks of light caused by particles from space called meteoroids. Meteoroids fall into the atmosphere at speeds of more than twenty-five miles per second. Friction with the Earth's atmosphere causes them to heat up and glow. The glowing light is the meteor.

Sporadic meteors are those that come from any direction at any time. We have no way of predicting when a sporadic meteor will appear. On a very clear, dark night, away from city lights, you may see ten per hour. Unlike sporadic meteors, meteor showers can be predicted. Meteoroids sometimes travel in large groups, called swarms. Many of these meteoroids are particles lost from a comet during its orbit around the sun. When the Earth crosses the comet's orbit, meteoroids enter the atmosphere and a meteor shower occurs. We can predict a shower because we know when the Earth will pass through a comet's trail. Some of the best meteor showers take place in August, when you may see up to fifty shooting stars an hour. Though the bright streaks look close together, they may be as far as 100 miles apart.

Meteoroids appear to move faster after midnight. This is due to the movement of the Earth in its orbit around the sun. When you look up at the early night sky, you are facing the direction Earth is moving away from. Meteoroids falling to Earth at that time must "catch up," and so appear slow. Towards the middle of the night, as the planet rotates, you are facing the direction the Earth is moving toward. Meteoroids in the sky appear to fall faster now, because you are racing toward them, not away from them.

During a meteor shower, you may see up to fifty shooting stars an hour streak through the sky.

Visitor From Space

On the morning of June 30, 1908, as the blazing sun rose over the Tunguska River in Siberia, another fireball suddenly raced into view. Witnesses said it was so bright it made the sunlight seem dim. Seconds later, there was an explosion that would later become known as the "Tunguska Event." The roar could be heard 600 miles away. Horses 400 miles away were knocked off their feet by the shock wave. Trees were leveled and blackened for twenty miles in all directions. One man claimed that heat from the blast had melted a set of knives and forks. When researchers finally arrived at the sight, there was no trace of whatever had caused the blast. Nor was there any sort of hole or crater. From the damage, though, it is clear the unknown object exploded with the force of a gigantic bomb.

Some very bizarre, even silly explanations have been given for the Tunguska Event. Some say the Earth was hit by a black hole from space, or blasted by a powerful ray from an alien spacecraft. Another idea is that an alien ship blew up while attempting to land. These theories make a good story, but the evidence points to an explosion of a comet or huge meteorite. The explosion must have occurred in the air. That is why no crater was ever found.

One clue supporting the comet theory was the appearance afterward of rare clouds in the evening sky. They are called *noctilucent* (nok·tih·LOOS·ent) clouds, which in Latin means "clouds that shine in the night." The upper rim glows with an eerie blue light. The underside shines a rich yellow-gold. They are the highest clouds in the atmosphere, forming about fifty miles up. Scientists think these clouds may be made of the dust and icy particles from comets.

A ball of fire brighter than the sun exploded near the Tunguska River.

Earth's Weirdest Weather

You've probably heard the saying "raining cats and dogs," but how about raining frogs and fish? A shower of fish fell in Glamorgan, Wales, on February 9, 1859. On June 16, 1882, the people of Dubuque, Iowa, were pelted with hailstones that had tiny frogs trapped inside. These unfortunate animals were probably sucked into the clouds from nearby streams and ponds by strong updrafts, then quickly frozen and covered with layers of ice. Frogs also fell on the town of Trowbridge, England, in 1939. They dropped onto the surprised townspeople during a summer rain.

After hearing about falling fish, falling snow may not seem odd. But what if it fell in the middle of the summer? In the United States, 1816 is known as the year without a summer. Across the northern states and Canada, heavy snow fell in June and people had to wear overcoats and mittens. On the Fourth of July, 1918, there weren't any fireworks in the Great Plains states. That morning began as a usual warm summer day, but soon it began to rain. As it became colder and colder, the rain turned into the snow of a summer blizzard that blasted the area for three days.

People complain about hurricanes, but did you know that a fierce hurricane once prevented a war? In 1889, German naval ships tried to take over the island of Samoa in the Pacific Ocean. They damaged American-owned property there and burned an American Flag. U.S. warships were sent. Before a battle could begin, however, a terrible storm struck. Ships were lost on both sides, and many sailors died. The islanders rushed to help drowning German and American sailors. Afterward, differences were settled with a peace treaty that same year.

A blizzard on the Fourth of July—
one of nature's tricks with our weather.

Tomorrow's Atmosphere

At one time, our ancestors believed that such things as the sun's journey from horizon to horizon, flickering lights in the sky, and the weather were all the work of gods or spirits. Now we know a great deal about what causes many of the wonders in our sky. Even more important, we are learning how to use that knowledge.

Predicting the weather helps people in many ways. Pilots use the information to enjoy safe journeys across the sky. Farmers need to know something about the weather to decide which crops to plant, and when. Knowledge of approaching storms helps to save lives and property.

We know now that certain measures must be taken to keep our air clean. Smog is a problem in many big cities, as is acid rain. Industrialized countries can send millions of tons of dust and gas such as carbon dioxide into the air every year. As a result, many scientists are concerned about the "greenhouse effect." This is a warming trend of the atmosphere, caused by too much carbon dioxide in the air. We are learning how to control and perhaps even correct the greenhouse effect and the problems of smog and acid rain. By carefully studying the wind conditions where factories are to be built, and by burning fuel more efficiently, we can help to prevent pollution. Planned use and conservation of our planet's great forests help to control carbon dioxide levels. By using wind and solar power—two very clean sources of energy provided by our atmosphere—we can lessen our dependency on more damaging forms of energy.

By taking the proper measures and using our resources wisely, we can be sure that tomorrow's generations, too, will be able to enjoy the wonders of the sky above.

For Further Reading

Branley, Franklyn M.: *Sundogs and Shooting Stars*, Boston, Massachusetts, Houghton Mifflin Co., 1980.

Branley, Franklyn M.: *It's Raining Cats and Dogs*, Boston, Massachusetts, Houghton Mifflin Co., 1987.

Bresler, Lynn: *Earth Facts*, Tulsa, Oklahoma, EDC Publishing, 1986.

Fradin, Dennis: *Disaster! Blizzards and Winter Weather*, Chicago, Illinois, Children's Press, 1983.

Gallant, Roy A.: *Rainbows, Mirages and Sundogs*, New York City, Macmillan Publishing, 1987.

Ganeri, Anita: *The Usborne Book of Weather Facts*, Tulsa, Oklahoma, EDC Publishing, 1987.

Knight, David C.: *The First Book of Deserts*, New York City, Franklin Watts, 1964.

Lavine, Sigmund: *Strange Travelers*, Boston, Massachusetts, Little, Brown & Co., 1960.

Purvis, George, and Purvis, Anne: *Weather and Climate*, New York City, Bookwright Press, 1984.

Slote, Alfred: *The Air in Fact and Fancy*, Cleveland, Ohio, World Publishing, 1968.

Index

Antarctica 29, 41
archaeopteryx 49
atmosphere 9, 11, 57
    carbon dioxide 7, 39, 62
    ionosphere 5
    first atmosphere 7
    stratosphere 5
    troposphere 5
auroras 5, 11

birds 5
    arctic tern 41
    cuckoo 47, 51
    flycatcher 51
    golden eagle 45
    hoatzin 49
    hummingbird 45
    weaverbird 47

clouds 7, 25, 29, 35
    cirrus 27
    cumulonimbus 21
    noctilucent 59
    thundercloud 13, 21,
        23, 31
comet 57, 59
cryoplankton 29
cyclone 35

doldrums 19
dust devil 33
dust storm 33

eggs
    of cuckoo 51
    of monarch butterfly 43
    of weaverbird 47
equator 19, 41

Fata Morgana 17
fog 37

greenhouse effect 62

hail 23, 61
horse latitudes 19

hurricane 35, 61

insects 5
    firefly 53
    glowworm 53
    monarch butterfly 43
    praying mantis 45

light 9, 11, 17, 27
lightning 13
    ball 15
    speed of 13
    St. Elmo's fire 15

magnetosphere 11, 41
Mars 7, 33
meteoroid 57, 59
migration
    of arctic tern 41
    of monarch butterfly 43
mirage 17
moon 27

ozone 5

photosynthesis 7
pollution
    acid rain 39, 62
    smog 37, 62

rain 21, 25, 33, 39, 61
rainbow 25

snow 33, 61
    snowflakes 29
sun 5, 7, 15, 19, 35, 41, 55
    halo 27
    solar power 62
    solar system 7, 55
    solar wind 11
    sundog 27
    sunlight 9, 25

Tornado Alley 31
Tunguska Event 59
typhoon 35

Waitomo Cave 53
weather 62
    blizzard 61
    fog 37
    hail 23, 61
    hurricane 35, 61
    lightning 13
    rain 29, 39, 61
    snow 29
    thunderstorm 21
    tornado 31
willy willie 35
wind 5, 21
    haboob 33
    hurricane 35, 61
    polar easterlies 19
    power 62
    prevailing westerlies 19
    tornado 31
    trade winds 19
    whirlwinds 33

zodiac 55
zodiacal light 55